NEW AND
SELECTED POEMS

Also by Edward Storey

Poetry

North Bank Night
A Man in Winter
The Dark Music
A Slant of Light
Last Train to Ely
A Change in the Climate

Prose

Portrait of the Fen Country
Four Seasons in Three Countries
The Solitary Landscape
Call it a Summer Country
Spirit of the Fens
Fen, Fire & Flood
The Winter Fens
Fen Country Christmas
In Fen-country Heaven
Letters from the Fens

Biography

A Right to Song: A Life of John Clare

Autobiography

Fen Boy First

Libretti

Katharine of Aragon (music by Barry Ferguson)
Old Scarlett (music by Trevor Hold)
No Cross, No Crown (music by David Twigg)
The Journey (music by David Twigg)

Edward Storey

New and
Selected Poems

Rockingham Press

Published in 2001
by
The Rockingham Press
11 Musley Lane,
Ware, Herts
SG12 7EN

British Library Cataloguing-in-Publication Data

A catalogue record for this book
is available from the British Library

ISBN 1 873468 80 6

Printed in Great Britain
by Biddles Limited, Guildford

Printed on Recycled Paper

eastengland | arts

For Angela

— the past, the present, and the whole.

The memory is that part of the present
which exposes the future ...

Bo Carpelan

True distance is not the concern of the eye,
it is granted only to the spirit.

Antoine Saint-Exupéry

Acknowledgments

To Chatto and Windus Ltd., who first published *NORTH BANK NIGHT* (1969) and *A MAN IN WINTER* (1972); Annakin Fine Arts for *THE DARK MUSIC* (1979); Free Man's Press for *A SLANT OF LIGHT* (1983); The Rockingham Press for *LAST TRAIN TO ELY* (1995) and *A CHANGE IN THE CLIMATE* (1997).

My thanks are also due to the following magazines or journals in which the new poems in this volume first appeared: *ACUMEN; A.E. HOUSMAN SOCIETY, BRANDO'S HAT, INTERPRETER'S HOUSE, THE MONTH, OPEN UNIVERSITY POETRY COMPETITIONS AND SHAKESPEARE SOCIETY, THE RIALTO* and *THE SWANSEA REVIEW.*

I also wish to express my gratitude to Dr. Jack Alster, Sean Body, David Twigg and especially my wife Angela, for their helpful suggestions towards compiling this representative selection from more than thirty years' work.

Contents

from **NORTH BANK NIGHT** *(1969)*

The Visit   10
In Memory of My Grandfather   11
Birthnight   12
The Return   13
The Carthorse Preacher   14
North Bank Night   16
Summer   17
South Creake   18
Visiting a Country Church   19
Hillside Burial   20

from **A MAN IN WINTER** *(1972)*

Fen Couple   21
Farm Hand   22
Celery Prickers   23
Rag-and-Bone-Man   24
Uncle   25
Neighbour   26
On Platform 5   27
Virago   28

from **THE DARK MUSIC** *(1979)*

Roads   29
The Wayfarer's Song   30
Mother   31
Making the Most of Autumn   32
Man and Winter   33
Song of a Church Visit with Schoolchildren   34
Message from the Asylum   36
Unauthorised Persons, Including Poets, Strictly Prohibited   37

from ***A SLANT OF LIGHT*** *(1983)*

John Clare Moves House 38
Clare's Last Meeting with Mary Joyce 39
Roots 40
Neighbours 41
Ploughman 42
To Emily Dickinson, from Ely 43

from ***A MEMORY OF POMEGRANATES*** *(1983-85)*
   previously unpublished
A Moment on Aegina 44
The Abandoned City 45
On Palaiochora 46
The Cockerels Will Not Let You Sleep in Olympia 47
In the Museum 48
No Ordinary Sailing 49
Eavesdropping at Perdika 50

from ***LAST TRAIN TO ELY*** *(1995)*

No Distances, No Grass 51
Beginner 52
I Think Today of One 53
Snap-shot 54
Smoke Signals 55
On the Way to a John Clare Society Committee Meeting 56
Ballad of the Railway-station Waiting-room 57
Pietà 60
Her Eyes Remain Cold Shadows 61
Three Poems on Edward Hopper Paintings 62

from ***A CHANGE IN THE CLIMATE*** *(1998)*

Foldings 65
Life-story 66
Death of an Uncle 68
The Inheritor 69
The Wireless Aerial 70
New Year's Eve – 1997 72

That Place, Those Hours 74
A Change in the Climate 75
War-cemetery – Poland 76
Good Friday – Spain 77
End of Term 78
Feeling Earth Pause 79
In an Alien Heaven 80
Experience 80

NEW POEMS (1999-2001)
First Things 82
A Mother Looking for Her Children 83
Visiting Hour 84
Feathers 85
Losers 86
Because of Life or Death 87
Shopping-Days 88
Two Miniatures 89
Look at Yourself 90
The Mirror 91
The Flitting 92
Credenhill 93
Closer to Ice than Fire 94
A Welsh Hill 96
A Valediction 98
A Ballad of Two Trees 100
Taking Down the Apple Tree 102
Neighbourhood Watch 103
Double Exposure 104
The Silence of Nantgwyllt 105
Elegy for a Rhondda Man 106
Portrait of an Artist 108
The Pales 110
Endgame 112

THE VISIT

I remember her annual coming,
her arms aching with blackberries,
a dead hare hanging from her wrist.
To me she came from a land where grass
lapped as the sea at her house,
where long and soft-eared animals
were carelessly caught, and trees
grew ancient as apples. Nothing changed.
Yearly she came with her thin voice
and dried-apricot face to be kissed.

Now, more than thirty years past,
I see my own mother enter our house,
her arms filled with a new summer
of plums and blackcurrants, her cheeks
lined with the part that now she plays.
Watching her thoughtful and tired eyes
gauging the impact of our joy
I feel surprised that we have shared
this casual acceptance of events –
the young and old at once familiar.

IN MEMORY OF MY GRANDFATHER

Swearing about the weather he walked in
like an old tree and sat down:
his beard charred with tobacco, his voice
rough as the bark of his cracked hands.

Whenever he came it was the wrong time.
Roots spread over the hearth, tripped
whoever tried to move about the room –
the house was cramped with only furniture.

But I was glad of his coming. Only
through him could I breathe in the sun
and the smell of fields. His clothes reeked
of the soil and the world outside.

Geese and cows were the colour he made them,
he knew the language of birds and brought them,
singing out of his beard, alive
to my blankets. He was winter and harvest.

Plums shone in his eyes when he rambled
of orchards. With giant thumbs he'd split
an apple through the core, and juice
flowed from his ripe, uncultured mouth.

Then, hearing the room clock chime,
he walked from my ceiling of farmyards
and returned to his forest of thunder.
The house regained silence and corners.

Slumped there in my summerless season
I longed for his rough hands and words
to break the restrictions of my bed,
to burst like a tree from my four walls.

BIRTHNIGHT

You wouldn't remember
thirty years ago, breaking
for the first time into the dim light
of a cramped bedroom.

It was a cold night
with earth suffering a severe winter.
Blinds kept from the prying stars
our room's hunger.

Your birth troubled no one.
I waited, quiet as the stairs
or poker-work text on the wall
or the new-born snow.

I felt joy at your coming.
Even when nerves stretched me to crying
and you seemed forever falling,
even to this world I hurried you.

Then suddenly all fire
let loose, more lights were lit,
and to our narrow lives you came
to wreck with cries our customary sleep.

THE RETURN

Little has changed.
The hot evening could, I am sure,
belong to any year. Men
with their shirt-sleeves rolled,
sit talking still outside their houses
or, tired with a hard day's work,
watch silently the martins' loud attempt
to break the speed record.

I know these terraced homes breed heat,
their stuffy bedrooms defy sleep.
So many generations here have kept
a truce with summer on their steps.
It is a common ritual that few
are willing to forget. They
pass their habits down like ornaments.

After the brickfields' burning day
they treasure these last cooling hours,
feeling the comfort on parched backs
of air that has not passed through fire.
They saw their fathers take this time
to let their blistered fingers breathe
and place calm evening on their eyes.

When I first left this clay-pit town
to find a different kind of work,
I thought ten years would see a change
but coming back from twice that time
it feels as if I changed my mind
and that same morning turned around.

THE CART-HORSE PREACHER

It would have been no use
using the smooth liturgical words
of a cosy religion.
His congregation left their work
in the wet fields of the fen-country,
their cracked hands swollen
with beet-chopping.

To have asked them into the stiff pews
of a cold church would have meant
shouting at air; he knew
the hollow stillness of that place
left them more frozen than the fields,
and holy whining more than winter
lined each face.

So he gathered them round him
on the market square, saying
'I'll speak a language you can understand.
Who cares about the use of lovely words
when half the words are nothing more than sound.'
Their frost-blue ears were tingled
by his fire.

They met him every Sunday night and knew
God would be called a muck-heap
or a cow, and no irreverence meant.
'Crops thrive', he'd say, 'where muck is spread,
and milk pumps life in every sucker's mouth.'
He solved the mystery of their fields,
healed their backs.

But now he's dead, and God's
locked in His church, stiff and alone.
Men work their days out on the land
wondering why the old cart-horse preacher
bothered them at all. Sometimes they feel
without him frost stays longer in their hands
and limbs more often ache.

NORTH BANK NIGHT

Tonight the cold air magnifies the sky,
loose nets of cloud are strung about the stars
and distant lights of cities rim the night
bright as the late owl's frosty claws.

Tonight the sky has space about its ears,
a million years from sun to blazing sun,
and darkness feels as tangible as fire
that burns the face and scars the ungloved hand.

Tonight the grass and hedges sweat with ice,
the river locks the stars behind its glass,
and that lone bird that swooped across the fields
is caught by hungry winter and devoured.

SUMMER

Removed from winter the sky blossoms.
Trees hatch from their black shells,
fledglings tremble like leaves trying to fly.

Over the water the fishing-rods of boys
make bars of music. Bream laze
in a minim of sunlight, and the stream

shimmers with cymbals. Hidden from gunsight
a fox sleeps in a boy's arms. Hares
leap through a forest of cornstalks.

Even the roads drowse out their long miles,
making earth shine with the bright beads
of their black sweat.

SOUTH CREAKE

for Anthony Scott

What violence will expose this peace
or shatter flame-light on cool stone?
Will the respect of ritual or myth
survive beyond the shadow of a faith?

This ancient tower stands against the rain
and darkness deepens with its mystery.
What wind-blown whistle through the grass
will flex the nerve and batter down those doors?

Hearing your music now within these walls,
watching completion of a thousand years,
sharing the silence of a candle's hour,
moves me again to this late questioning.

Within the chancel burns a light,
and thoughts of incense fill my mind
with dying hyacinths in a room
where I had peace of yet another kind.

Pale shadows weave upon the floor
image and dream and those poor fantasies
that filled my discontented blood.
Now I could lose all those idolatries,

all those ambitions and inflated songs
within one anthem in this ageless night.
Outside, a dog howls through the storm.
Your music stops. The silent pillars wait.

VISITING A COUNTRY CHURCH

We talked for a long time to the old vicar
hunched in his brown, unsanctimonious coat,
listening as his quiet Yorkshire voice
spent itself freely on our willing ears.

Before he saw us standing in the aisle
we'd watched his simple care for how things looked –
the laundered altar-cloth, the vase of flowers,
the glint of sunlight on cleaned brass –
an old man putting his house in order
for tomorrow's few.
                              Yet this was more than ritual.
Talking about the windows of clear glass
we noticed then his weariness of eyes,
his frail and breaking syllables of hope.

Here was no proud and holy-acting priest
with condescending graces and cool charm,
but a conscientious saint in common dress,
himself worn-out with those twin tasks
of praying for the souls of his indifferent flock
and raising seventy thousand pounds
to save the steeple for their wedding days.

HILLSIDE BURIAL

Between the dry stone walling of a hill
twelve men are burying a neighbour,
their bare heads barren as boulders,
their throats brittle as dead heather.

There is no priest, ceremony, flowers,
only the shepherds' granite words
committing one of their own kind
to the dark field beyond earth's boundary.

And as they lock his body from the sun
with soil and pebbles of his native land,
each feels the emptiness and loss
left in their fingers by the falling stone.

FEN COUPLE

I see them again,
brother and sister
sharing for seventy years
the same sad fire.

Encamped in their damp
corner of the room
they watch their garden
under perennial frost.

She could have done better,
letting fastidious hands
loose on a house,
but never with him.

Content to stare
at the starved grate
he has spent his life
twiddling years round his thumbs.

And so they endure,
eking care out like coal,
growing in misery
more in debt to each other.

FARM HAND

I would have portrayed you once
as part of the rich character
of these fields, your ponderous limp
a product of the black soil, the split
roots of your hands wealthy as muck.

I would have dressed you in words
to keep out the raw winds of your life,
would have made you spectacular
as the sun rising in winter, or as part
of a landscape by Brueghel the elder.

But that would have gilded
your rank flower, would have disguised
the exhausted bud of your eyes
and silenced the loud ache
of your bones' arthritis.

For someone's gain you have banged
your head on a sky of indifference.
You have grown old cursing the fields
for survival – a byproduct of wealth,
defying description.

CELERY PRICKERS

You say too easily
there's virtue living near the soil.

Those women crawling on all-fours
pricking-out celery plants would not agree.

For them there is no comfort in a cold east wind
whipping their broad backsides all day.

Even the canvas screen around each bed
cannot protect them from the black wet earth.

The only profit they get from the land
comes once a week to fatten each tight purse.

Watching them from the comfort of a car
you might compare their stitchery of plants

with that more gentle art of tapestry,
seeking some finery that is not there.

But stand outside and feel their bawdy talk
suck such glib thoughts from your unseasoned roots.

RAG-AND-BONE-MAN

This is where he lived,
the rag-and-bone man
who rifled my spare dreams.

In this yard he cursed
among bedsteads and fenders
the poor harvest of scrap

and thin autumn of brasses.
Chains rattled. Rain
rusted on mangles.

I remember his fence
and the walls of his shed
heavy with hare skins,

among them the sad fur
of my own rabbit – killed
for our Sunday table –

its coat cold, the care
of my days strung up
for a few pence.

I hated that warped man
whose iron claws could
snatch from my small hands

the soft warmth of my pride
and give in return
the damp grief of his coins.

UNCLE

At last we have taken that picture down.
For more than twenty years his photograph
has looked out from our chimney-breast,
his calm, unblinking eyes watching us,
his regimental badge permanently bullshone.

As children we accepted his grey face
as part of the furniture, his fixed smile
hiding the fear of war – the khaki lie
of a young man nailed up on our wall,
pretending he was a soldier.

Three days later he was killed in France,
(or was he drowned? I just forget).
All I remember are the days of questioning,
the tears on faces I had not seen cry,
and then that enlarged photograph.

And now it's down what can we find
to put there in its place? A coloured print
of our own children and their wedding days?
Or something from our holiday in Wales?
Or should we leave the nail for next year's calendar?

NEIGHBOUR

This neighbour-soldier found his death
in a delayed Flanders, with no sound
of shouting, bugles, gunfire.

After forty years nursing a proud wound
he died in a suburban house,
rarely called on by friends or relations.

Rising to reveille he fell one day
and gashed his head upon the grate.
There was no witness, no trooper's comforting.

Lying stiff and bloody in his no-man's-land
he did not near the milkman slam the gate,
the postman shove a gas-bill through the door.

Police came, then cousins, and the corpse
was carted away like an old couch.
  Since then the room's had many visitors.

ON PLATFORM 5

I watch you gripping your hands
that have grown into the familiar contours
of old age, waiting for the train
to begin its terrifying journey
back to yourself, to your small house
where the daily habit of being alone
will have to be learnt all over again.

Whatever you do with your lined face
nothing disguises that look in your eyes.
Between you and your family
words push like passengers until
your daughter kisses you goodbye –
uttering those parting platitudes
that spill about the closing of a door.

For them your visit's over and relief
jerks in the hands half-lifted now to wave.
Soon there will be far distances between
and duty letters counting out your year.
A whistle blows. The station moves away.
A magazine stays clenched upon your lap.
And your white knuckles tighten round each fear.

VIRAGO

After the exaggerations about your fierce tongue
I was prepared for the claw-scratching of your spite,
ready for the wrath and fire they said would pour
out of the sour volcano of your soul.

Then you came in, a forgotten cobweb
undisturbed in the world's mind for a hundred years,
no lava spilling from your mouth, no scorn,
only unspoken questions as we held your hands.

As we were carefully explained and named
I watched you thumb through albums of your brain
trying to recognise this woman who was child
in those starched-linen years where faces never change.

I watched you stare beyond the valley's rain
to where the fading coal-tips aged with moss,
sinking your shaft of thought deep down to comprehend
why I'd outgrown the age my mother was.

Poor ghost, poor fragile remnant of yellowing lace,
are you that wild virago of your family's talk?
If so, they should come back to see you as you are,
your mind burnt out while theirs rage in the dark.

ROADS

Here there is always a long way to go.
The roads do not encourage you into
deceptive corners or an enticing ridge
as they do in hill-country. On this edge
of earth's platform they beckon beyond
a few trees or farmhouse, separating a land
that sulks below sea-level. Look any way
and these roads narrow towards the sky,
towards that space where the clouds grow.
You can take these roads at their face value,
they have nothing to hide and what you cannot see
is beyond the boundary of the naked eye.

You may feel that a man's stature should be measured
by his landscape, his bones hard, his fissured
brow a replica of the rock's forehead,
the contours' rhythm caught in his stride.
Not here. A man gauges his worth against
intemperate winds, feeling his face rinsed
by the rain flung in from the sea. He works
not by stone walls but by those open dykes
where rats nest in the soft peat, and eels
slip through the dark stream like a vague thought.
You can hate these roads or find, like hills,
they lift you, step by step, out of the soul's drought.

THE WAYFARER'S SONG

I would go back now to the axe-ring
and the aching round in the wood's being –
footstep and armstroke in the daily need
of fire and shelter. Should this be denied
in the last hours I would lose all that the blood
has journeyed for. Bruised by the cold winds
of a love's winter a worn man should be
where the roots are, where the tree-rings
are those of his father's father. And when eyes close
sweet music should come, like the smell of wood
to the wood-cutter's nostrils to comfort his soul.

Of all things that call me back to the tribe's ground,
to the grip of tongues and primitive sounds
providing fire, it is the rhythm of songs sung
in the feeble light of a family evening
when questions brood on familiar faces.
A man knows then when his ambitions have faded,
when women fail to quicken the heart-beat and lust ceases.
Melody comes from the longings of man,
from the dreams that have drawn him, kept him
beyond mountains in an alien landscape,
studying stones more than stars for his horoscope.

I would go back to the rhythm of seasons and singing,
to the rhythm of axe-ring and labour,
of cradle and water, hearthside and harbour.
A man knows his landfall when the journey is over,
sees in the firelight the spent flames of the lover.
That plain girl with her straight hair, bringing
water in a chipped horn and her first bread,
is better by far than those silken women
in once-travelled kingdoms. The rhythm of sleep
and the rhythm of voices, these are the virtues
to prize when each weary eye closes.

MOTHER

Watching you wind the clock
that has ticked on your wall
for fifty years my mind goes back
to that tiny room when my bed
stood near a bright coal fire
both day and night, where in the dark
you sang by the fire-flame's light
as a fever lifted my body up
to float in the air above my sheets –
a simple song born out of fear
but sustained by a deeper faith
and the need to keep yourself awake.

More than enough history
has taken place since prayer
and your safer hands helped break
death's tow-rope on my body then,
but watching you check
the rhythm of that ageing pendulum
I hear again your voice
rocking my heart to sleep
in constant chimes of love
that did not lose, unwind, or stop,
giving both child and mother hope
through those long hours of dark.

MAKING THE MOST OF AUTUMN

The light stretches a long way today
pushing the clouds to other continents,
and fields look twice their size because the sun
touches horizons twenty miles away.

Black furrows merge towards a stranded house
shining like some bright spider in its web.
Potato-pickers on a distant farm
could be wildflowers bending in the wind.

A tractor pulls a parachute of gulls
to check its landing-speed before it turns
to plough new flights of soil, while in the sky
larks make again a rainbow of bright sound.

And in backyards, or on some new estate,
greenhouses flash with rich chrysanthemums
giving the day such things to celebrate
that winter dares not come to spoil earth yet.

MAN AND WINTER

For the first time this winter
the fields are salted with frost,
the black soil silent again
after the chant of the plough
and white procession of gulls.

Nearby a man blows into his hands
renewing the habit that will last a season.
It is not prayer that comforts
the cold ache of his flesh but breath
warmed with his own fire.

The distance is brought nearer by mist
which seldom deserts this land
during days that hardly get started.
You need to be different to work these fields,
it's almost a calling.

Men meet times like this with blood
that has tested the worst of each year.
They too are salt, earning more
than their keep and the sun's bonus,
paying more than a rent to be part of the earth.

SONG OF A CHURCH VISIT
WITH SCHOOLCHILDREN

We sat in an upturned boat
beached on the shores of Spring,
with flowers bright as angel-fish
and light on the polished wing
of a bird in a cage of colour
where winds made the rain-bells ring.

We sat where the timbers arched
their wish-bone shapes above,
a wooden spire for our keel
and the eagle for the dove
in search of a singing rainbow
with words as warm as love.

We listened to a story
older than ship or crown
of *Mary, Mary Magdalene* *
who threw a pebble down
to grant each lucky child a wish
in that distant, salty town.

We listened to the weather
outside our stranded ark
and heard a thousand voices
speaking from the dark
and fading stones of history
where the living seldom talk.

There were robbers' graves around us
on which grass never grows,
and a lost princess who slumbers
where no noisy ocean flows
tugging at sea-weed bell-ropes
when the March wind blows.

34

There were graves of unknown children,
names nibbled away by moss,
and a tree the shape of an anchor
and a man on the mast of a Cross
who was killed one stormy Easter,
stretched out like an albatross.

We sat while the day turned over
and the words spilt from each hand
and the fish went back to flowers
and the water turned to sand,
and our upturned boat became a church
as we sailed back to land.

But when these creaking timbers
crack and fall to dust,
when the coloured port-holes crumble
and the cabin hinges rust,
who will come here, I wonder,
to listen and think of us?

*   *Mary, Mary Magdalene* is a reference to the poem by
Charles Causley.

MESSAGE FROM THE ASYLUM

They're at it again, poking about in my soul,
telling the world why I am here, or rather
why I should not be here. But they'd soon
change their tune if they had been through
what I have been through.

There are times when I'd like to go back
to my family, but going back is
harder than you think. And when I see
how mad the world has gone I must admit
that I've been grateful for these twenty years
away from it. I've been looked after,
well fed, kept free from lice
and all responsibilities.

The only drawback has been no women.
I have missed not having their thighs
in which to hide my breaking head
when the world's been poking about in my soul.

And now they have cut off my head,
picked out all the letters of the alphabet,
all the vowels and consonants, and brought them
out through my ears. Then they tell me
to write poetry. *The fools!*

They've decided too that I did not know
Lord Byron and the bard from Warwickshire.
If they won't believe me why don't they
stop poking about in my soul?
I feel sometimes like telling them
to stuff my poems ... LEAVE ME ALONE!

But then, perhaps, I should go mad
were I not talked about and popular.

UNAUTHORISED PERSONS, INCLUDING POETS, STRICTLY PROHIBITED

Dear Clare, you really would go mad
if you could come back now
to your own country. Your
favourite woods are gone completely
and the spinneys are protected by guard-dogs.

You would find it a strange landscape
with arrogant signs jabbing
at eyeballs – KEEP OUT!
BEWARE OF ALSATIONS! UNAUTHORISED
PERSONS STRICTLY PROHIBITED!

Yes, and that includes poets,
anyone in fact who would
like to walk through a field
or search near the roots of a hedge
to find the first primrose.

You remember Swordy Well, Royce Woods
and Helpstone Heath? Then remember,
for they exist now only in the memory
and the bright words picked by you
one morning when no one was looking.

JOHN CLARE MOVES HOUSE

They have brought me to a new house
with larger grounds and a small rent,
believing that song needs no more
than a warm hearth or a field with a cow.
But since she whom I love is no longer here
how can my heart sing or pen give wings
to the sick bird in my breast? Song needs more
than five acres of land and a thatched roof.

The fields too are bare of the flowers
I knew on Emmonsails Heath, and the stream
limps with its burden of cloud through the dark fen.
Charity does not beget song,
nor do the good intentions of those
who know better the comforts of wealth.
Without love walls can only be walls
and the nightingale dead.

CLARE'S LAST MEETING
WITH MARY JOYCE

Because I could not stay you had to go,
walk off alone along the empty street,
the way too many lovers have to know.

I saw how eyes of sorrow then could show
a grief that only dying makes complete;
because I could not stay you had to go.

And there was death without the death-bell's slow
and public noise declaring beat by beat
the way too many lovers have to know.

I held your hands and felt the good years flow
like blood from wounds no healing could defeat.
Because I could not stay you had to go.

I watched you turn and saw your head bend low;
this was the moment time would not repeat –
the way too many lovers have to know.

And then I stood alone where fen winds blow
across the fields where we would often meet.
Because I could not stay you had to go.

I found a refuge where deep waters flow
with all our secrets and let madness cheat
the way too many lovers have to know.

But you, my dear, could only let grief grow
until the bell was silent, earth discreet.
Because I could not stay you had to go,
the way too many lovers have to know.

ROOTS

What makes a man belong to a place?
A house, an accent, or a piece of land?
An entry in a register of names
which states that where he lives
is where he now belongs? What else?
A street, a town, a blade of grass,
or something as familiar as a face
that stares each morning from a looking-glass?

Crumble the soil, fork down beneath
the footprints of these later years
and you will find the roots unsevered
where a child received first air,
then sky, then spaces all around,
and that essential rhythm in the blood
which says 'This place is home,
this modest land is good.'

Today I met a man who shares
my fascination with these fields.
He said, 'It is not what you see
but what you know. Each furrow
is a lifeline on the hand. Each reed
a symbol of our ancestry.' I stand
and, in the silence, hear again
familiar voices rising from the ground.

NEIGHBOURS

Next door my neighbours are listening
to their radio. Music so faint I strain
my hearing to enjoy the distance now
that separates their world from mine.

And something in the fragments that I hear
brings back a moment when this room was shared,
when we had music played so quietly
that only we knew what was heard.

But now this room is silent, and outside
dry leaves are shuffling round the gate
like prying children trying to get in.
The house by memory is made desolate.

The moment is as sharp as any thorn
exposed by winter. In such frail moods
I dare not move for fear the thought is torn.
I dare not speak in case the silence bleeds.

PLOUGHMAN

He had it all to himself
ploughing alone in a field
the size of a continent.

There was the day's new warmth,
the unexpected light
released from a cold sky.

Even the gulls did not find him,
and larks ventured too high
to be part of his earth.

He owned that remarkable space
not to be found in cities
or where hills brood.

He went out and came back
all day on the long wake
of his own sailing,

a monotonous journey
with only sleep and a ploughed field
for his destination.

There will be other days
when the rain will try out its nails
on his parched face,

when the undisciplined wind
will blunt every wave
of his black sea,

but these he will patiently bear
rather then turn into our world
where there are no seasons.

TO EMILY DICKINSON, FROM ELY

Here, bright wren,
where your father's fathers lived,
you would have had the same friends –
your dog, and the sundown dwarfing the grey
cathedral your ancestors would have known;
but no hills, and no one in the neighbourhood
taking you seriously.

I did not know,
girl of the sherry-hued eyes
and chestnut hair, that you and the Fens
had this much in common, but who else
could have described with such irony
the behaviour of mortals – whether at Amherst
or among these ancestral strangers?

There are times
when I see the lace-curtains of the sky
pulled to one side that I imagine you
at your immortal window, smiling,
secretly writing another masterpiece
to put with all those packets neatly stored away
for other eyes than those of relatives and countrymen.

A MOMENT ON AEGINA

I remember her now
in a white headscarf
blouse and pale mauve skirt.

How could I violate her stillness
with a camera-click, or stare too long
at what compelled such awe?

Whenever I recall that hour
held in the broken ribs of a temple
I think of her weeping for a land

worn-out with its past,
where neither cypress nor pomegranate
redeemed what came close to perfection.

Walking away I knew
that the moment I'd lost
was the moment I should have kept.

Now I can never be sure
if she was the ghost of Aphaia
or a lonelier girl who sat

on those crumbling stones and wept.

THE ABANDONED CITY

This is where the women and children screamed all night
when their men were taken and brutally slaughtered.

The guide-book says their voices could be heard
pleading across the valley to Aphaia's shrine.

So why, in this world of deities and saints
were there no gods to hear their cries - *COVER US! COVER US!*

Today a peasant woman sits outside
the Church of Episkopi, listening to her radio.

On her lap a piece of crochet, grubby with old age,
and at her feet four mangy cats asleep.

She beckons us inside, points to the water in a well, and says –
For sick, see ... You drink and never will be ill ...

We drink, fearing we never will be well again,
then stare at paintings on the walls and roof.

Those saints remain as silent now as when
the unheard women soaked this hill with blood.

ON PALAIOCHORA

Where, then, are the dead on this hill of the dead,
or the bones of the many who died
when these stones were a city?

Eyes can discern the pattern of streets
from cobbles in grass, but where
is their cemetery?

If any graves exist they must be
these small churches clinging to grey rocks,
each one a sepulchre.

Inside, one half expects to find
the body of a still unrisen Christ,
his wounds unhealed.

The only trappings left today
are broken icons, incense-lamps
and burnt-out candles fossilized in sand.

In one, an empty whisky bottle
hints at other solaces –
some quick guilt's ease to fill the cup of prayer.

Now only drunken bees
continue chanting in and out of walls
where faded paintings serve to prove

that praying is best done with active hands.

THE COCKERELS WILL NOT
LET YOU SLEEP IN OLYMPIA

For a few days everything went back to a beginning.
Cockerels made declarations from village yards
long before stars faded beyond cypresses.

He was luckier who could not sleep for the nightingales
in Platres. Our birds raucoused reveille
as if to prophesy the birth of some new god.

Donkeys brayed on hills as they once did in fables,
goat-bells scrambled as water down barren rocks
and the sky was a blood-soaked bandage.

Beyond cock-crow, shadows moved in the empty Stadium
and there were echoes of men who could not ignore
even the trumpeters' ghost-calls.

Were they the true gods – those men who ran naked
for their honour in front of an admiring woman
who had failed in deception? Times do not change.

Rub the dust from your eyes. Smell the oil
from the olive groves. We live in an age where
the cockerels will not let you sleep in Olympia.

IN THE MUSEUM

The bronze of a young charioteer,
whose face betrays the mystery of success,
looks down at us with wry bewilderment.

Why do we stare? What killings
made him popular and brought this crowd
to share his doubtful victories?

Fame offers strange memorials –
a statue in a market-place, a street,
a multi-storey carpark, or a lie.

History writes its own biographies.
Those crumbling busts of marble only show
what someone thought of someone long ago.

We stand before Poseidon who,
buried for twenty centuries beneath the sea,
now rules a civic room, as sad as Lear.

Each vein, each muscle, strains
to prove that gods were mightier then men.
The charioteer looks on, bemused, unsure.

What gave him honour is no longer true,
his silent eyes pretend to look away
from where great thrones collapse into the sea.

NO ORDINARY SAILING

We sat by the harbour wall
remembering when we first sailed to this island.
Among the passengers were olive-coloured men
who sang in guttural voices, their songs old as rocks.

Words rose and fell to the ship's roll,
phrases snatched by the wind and returned to the hills –
sad melodies that echoed the sea, deep
with Time's underflow. It was for us no ordinary sailing.

Then by the harbour steps we saw
dead fish like entrails gleaming in green water.
It was a contradiction in a land where all is thought
to be immortal, as if creation's purpose was held back.

Along the wall sat men who could have been
those chosen on the shores of Galilee – Andrew, James
and Simon Peter – mending their nets
and wondering where the best catch would be found that night.

Hard to believe their young impulsive choice
once left old neighbours bitter with regret.
At noon a solemn bell began to toll
and round the harbour sleep pulled down its blinds.

EAVESDROPPING AT PERDIKA

(a middle-aged American talks to a restaurateur)

My daughter phoned yesterday
from Seattle and said
'when are you coming home?'

I told her, 'Who knows?
Maybe I'll never be back.
I guess I'm finding peace of mind out here.'

Can you understand that?
I'm beginning to feel there are times
when we're not even in charge of our own lives.

My wife died last Fall
and I couldn't stay there alone,
not where everything had been shared.

Then my job came to an end
and I thought the best thing to do
was to get away from it all.

I'm getting used to it here.
My pension goes much further
and I'm not even sure now what is reality.

'My friend,' said the restaurateur,
'the moment you think about reality
you cannot take life seriously any more.'

You're right. Take a place like this.
It's kinda healing, yet unreal,
you know what I mean –

grief, wine, being alone,
all mixed up with other people's history …
You're lucky. You're already home.

NO DISTANCES, NO GRASS

Within our boundaries was world enough.
Earth had no frontiers we wished to cross.
The fields upheld us and each daily sun
decided always where adventure was.

We watched our fathers working on the land,
the farmers' trailers wilting under corn;
then mothers in coarse aprons and large hats
riddling potatoes near an open barn.

We saw the seasons marry and unfold
through habit, ritual, or commonsense.
There was no need to question or explain
the narrow streets or meadows' bright expanse.

But when the gates were opened and the town
let half its children out to go abroad,
we lost our freedom and the skies closed in
like walls we could not climb or then break down.

The world was suddenly too small and old,
there were no distances, no grass, no air.
The furrows, rivers, games and days of light
were in a country we had known elsewhere.

As exiles then we told ourselves that we
were driven out like tenants with bad debts,
when what we know is that we chose to go
and being wrong is what we can't accept.

BEGINNER

Sometimes I think I hear the thud of your spade
striking into the mud with the slow beat
of a dying heart – a death-bell's measured stroke
tolling under a dark sky for the end of an old earth.

Each mile of dyke is a grave for that dour breed
who inhabited England – dwellers of the true Fens
where mere and reed-bed, eel and bittern,
were holy relics in a land no man had conquered.

I also hear the guttural accent of your voice
as you curse the day you were brought to work
in this kingdom of ague and mist, where men
tore out your eyes or broke your back for another's sake.

The laments you gathered from the hills, the songs
learnt from the seas, still weigh on your tongue.
I feel the longing for what you will never regain,
the sad blood mourning for a stolen house.

But all histories pass and the seed of your seed
flourished under the uninhibited skies
of a country fashioned by man's sweat –
water to water, ash to ash, flower and root.

Yet night and the silence can never forget
the resentment you felt in your labourer's chains,
or the peculiar weave of eccentric fate
that made a virtue of your unwritten elegies.

I, who am last of the first of that ken,
sing now for the sake of the land you won –
rivers out of the flood, gold from the earth,
and of days unfettered by a master's wrath.

I THINK TODAY OF ONE

I think today of one who
even before her childhood was quite done
worked in the fields in frost and sun
from day's first light until the moon
sent labourers home, the girls
to mend torn garments in a lamp-lit room
made private by the pulling down of blinds.

Then, when the cockerels called
or neighbours knocked upon her window-pane,
she went with others just as young
back to the farm, her slender form
ill-matched for such long toil,
having no time to watch the tall
slow cumulus or hear the skylark's dirl.

And yet through her I love this land
where less appeals to unperceiving eyes
than what I find. I know I take
the aches and elements at second-hand
and should regret that she
was forced by circumstance to break
her spirit where I forge my song. But who

will understand the meaning of my
labours now unless they honour hers?
She would be quick to contradict
my pity and explain in simple terms
that others had fared worse.
She kept her thoughts like secrets in a house
where sorrows should be patched behind closed doors.

SNAP-SHOT

Was she that young, once? If only
I could breathe on the photograph
and bring her back to life, make water move
and ripple round her feet, she might
step out to prove she was a girl who
liked to laugh and run along the beach,
slender as grass and gossamer-light;
each day a gift – wife, mother, daughter
caught by the camera many tides ago
when holidays were brief and summers won
out of long months of servitude.

Why is it when we see ourselves
as children, our parents look no younger
than today – as if we are the only ones
who grow, while they stay ageless, until
a certain moment shatters that calm pose
and suddenly the sea, smiles, years,
dry-up into these wrinkles of tired skin
that now hang loosely on the bone
and can so easily be bruised
when memory no longer drugs with lies
and pictures hurt as only home-truths can?

SMOKE SIGNALS

My father, who'd not smoked for forty years,
sat on his death-bed puffing mock cigars
and blowing smoke-rings down the midnight ward
like tiny haloes flying without wings.

He did not speak but smiled and gently waved
at someone opposite who was not there.
The pain had left him as his mind returned
to days when he was young, with strength to spare.

Within his tight-skinned skull already cold
he felt the sun and heard the laughing sea
where he'd gone paddling on his one week off,
his work-day trousers rolled up to the knee.

I tried to talk but something in my throat
choked back the words for I was now a child
clutching his hand as I did then, afraid
of what might happen should I lose my hold.

I watched his fingers stiffen round my own,
his staring eyes withdraw, the smoke-rings fade.
And, in the low-lit ward beyond his death,
felt the first shudder of the turning tide.

ON THE WAY TO A COMMITTEE MEETING OF THE JOHN CLARE SOCIETY

I saw an old man sitting on a stone
beside a five-barred gate, his wild eyes
staring through me as I passed, as if
I had no right to cross a world
he'd fenced with private boundaries.

His gaze had hints of madness like a fire
raked by the wind. His bulbous head
(too big for what was left of him)
crimson with threats of anger or
some vision that was burning deep inside.

The first impression was of some daft clown
turned out of house to spend the afternoon
on country roads, out of harm's way. But then
I thought he might have chosen to be there
rather than waste his presence on the sane.

Wild flowers were his company, the fields
his joy. And, for a moment, I believed
I'd seen a poet sitting by that gate.
I would have stopped the car, gone back to look ...
but in my heart I knew it was too late.

BALLAD OF THE RAILWAY-STATION WAITING-ROOM

(for Trevor Hold)

We met, as strangers often do, and talked as friends.
He, hoping to make some kind of journey back;
I, having to travel forward, yet both
the reluctant passengers of fate.

It's dark in here, he said, *and cold. What time's
your train?* I could not give a definite reply –
Today, tomorrow, or a year to come.
(I was not used to such uncertainty.)

He shook his head. *It's been the same with me,
I've waited twenty years to go back home;
hopes raised, lies told, the broken promises;
and all the silences when no one came.*

I noticed then how grey the bare walls were.
A sheet of pegboard plugged the empty grate,
and there were smells of stale tobacco smoke
from others who, before us, had to wait.

Where are you from? he asked. Not far, I said.
We might have been close neighbours once
had years not intervened. I too have walked
the fields you knew, trod the same country lanes.

He did not answer that. The light grew darker still.
It was the kind of evening that is permanent;
a gloomy place with no one to explain
why both our trains were late – delayed, postponed.

And did you love the woman that I loved? he asked.
It's possible, I said, if we dispense with time.
His wild eyes looked beyond the window-pane –
there is no time in here, no calendar, no clocks.

All time is eternity. I've written that somewhere.
Now I am dead and longing to go back
to where I lived, while you are wishing
you could always stay where earth is kind –

the Fens, you said? Not quite what I would choose.
I found my pleasure in those ancient hills
near Barnack, where the yellow stones
grew green and mellow in an autumn sun.

I tried to say it wasn't flatness I so much admired
as space and light. I longed for fields and sky
unhindered by the boundaries of man.
I sought horizons that could not be reached.

He laughed: *Always the unattainable!*
The one thing that I've learnt in my long life
is that one never should out-grow
what's measured by the cloth of one's own birth.

But what of fame? I asked. You have known that.
Did that not compensate for what the world
saw as your lack of privilege? There was reproach
and sadness in his slow reply: *I thought you knew,*

a burden comes with every song we write.
No praise or flattery is worth the price
we pay for stepping out of paradise.
I had a mind that once was full of light

until the stars were driven from my head
by those who claimed they understood

58

and, for my safety, locked me up ... He paused,
and then, as if I were not there, began to sing:

Do letters reach beyond the grave?
Which wind will take them there?
Shall I rely upon the worms
to whisper in your ear?

Or shall I tell that secret bird
the words I could not say
when we walked by the riverside
before the grief of snow?

If I could send these pages
by wing, or fire, or tree,
would you believe at last, my dear,
those unsaid words were true?

And should you share that company
where sorrows are unknown,
you'd know why I was silent ...
Can such a love be sin?

Then, as his ghostly song came to an end,
four men stepped in with solemn tread
and stood before him as he wept: 'Your train
is coming, Mr Clare. Pick up your hat!

He turned and waved a fragile hand:
It won't be long, he said. *Remember, time*
is in the mind, like pain or joy, or love;
we only ever mourn for what we cannot have.

They put him in his box, they carried him away.
I sensed a sudden chill where he had sat.
Then, knowing that I was alone again,
felt the cold hands of fear about my throat.

PIETÀ

(from a bronze by Käthe Kollwitz)

The man returns as a child
to rest within the thighs from which he came;
his legs bent double, his head thrown back,
as helpless as a creature newly born.

The mother's pain is greater at his death
than anything she felt at birth.
Then the fulfilment eased her suffering
and no one saw the star shaped as a cross.

Today her grief is burdened
with the apparent failure of a dream,
sobs heaving with the sorrow of a heart
asking repeatedly 'What have they done?'

She aches to take him back
into herself, the first fruit of her womb
lying so bruised and lifeless in her lap,
till loneliness itself becomes a wound.

All she can be is the warm cradle
in which his body sleeps – a woman
rocking her baby through the night;
her tears falling as balm upon his brow.

HER EYES REMAIN COLD SHADOWS

(from a sketch by Käthe Kollwitz)

More shadows than light
because some greys are always permanent.

Corners fill out the room,
the day is still a paler shade of night.

A woman sits the other side of hope
staring into the ashes of a dream.

Upon the table is a knife,
and on a chair-back hangs a waiting rope.

What burden could be worse
than being a poor woman, mother, wife?

Her flesh is bloodless,
each dry breast folded like an empty purse.

But somewhere in the dark
a child sleeps on. A husband prays for work.

Where there is life ... How trite!
Her eyes remain cold sorrows. Memories mock.

Where is the wine of love,
the promised comfort of the broken bread?

She cups her hands to grieve,
to drown the cries of hunger in her head.

THREE POEMS ON EDWARD HOPPER PAINTINGS

1. A Middle-aged Couple

Her dreams are now in a book,
his on the empty railway track
outside their room. Once
they were shared and ran towards
a common meeting-place long since
unmet – their travelling marred
by incidents unplanned, each
settling for a station they could reach.

She sits, half-dressed. He stands
close to the window for his cigarette.
There is no hurry for the middle-aged.
They wait and think about what was
or is – a something in between
that both unites and separates.
There's always time to dress, undress,
accept, reject, adjust to loneliness.

She turns the pages slowly. He
glances at the ash held in his hand.
Another night, day, journey done,
another hotel room, the jug
of water stale now on its stand.
No need for explanations.
Once more on walls the shadows prove
the sun remains outside, like love.

2. Office Clerk

A man sits at his empty desk
staring out at the day's light.
It's not the future that he sees
but rather the past – all that might
have been if only the first risk
had been taken. There are no trees
on the skyline, only the flat
rooftops in a shaded street –
and all those questions windows make us ask.

The walls are bare. Even the sun
succeeds only in leaving a square
of blankness where no shadows fall.
There is no other being there,
no laughter heard, no movement seen,
only the silence of a tall
building when everyone has gone.
Yet he remains, brooding alone,
knowing the key of darkness will turn soon.

3. The Chair

If this chair were suddenly vacant
everything would still be there
except the girl sitting by the window –
the table with its vase of flowers
nearest the light; the velvet cloth
neatly arranged by hand; the blinds
partly pulled down to shade the sun.

Across the street the houses would sleep on
throughout the drowsy afternoon,
each secret life hidden in shadow.
Even the chair would still exist,
a piece of furniture within a room
full of its former presences, as if
it waited for the girl's return.

Perhaps there's no such thing as emptiness
but varying degrees of light and shade
that hide, reveal, like curtains drawn
to separate us from the world outside.
In every stillness there must be
something we cannot touch but only feel,
for when we look again the chair *is* occupied.

FOLDINGS

Our two hands had not touched like that
since fifty years ago I helped her fold
the white sheets from the washing-line.
Starting apart we shook each one
from head to foot, from left to right,
until it shortened and our hands
met like the hands of those who meet
in stately order at a dance.

You take your end, I'll take mine.
Fold and double-fold, don't let go.
It was a ritual that made
each Monday-morning Reckett's-blue
and taught me innocently of love.
Now she lies white with hands that will
not tug or pull at sheets again,
or shorten longer distances.

With her late death a childhood dies
and there's no point in asking questions now.
Nor can my words begin to tell
the double grief I feel.   The path
where once we stood and laughed
is gone; but somewhere I still hear –
You take your end, I'll take mine.
Fold and double-fold, don't let go.

LIFE-STORY

Daybreak: and I see you rising for work,
rummaging through the last shadows of sleep
before creeping downstairs and into the street
on your way to the farm. The first one up,
the last to bed. Each mile from the town
the only chance you'd have to yourself,
to dream it might have been different once.
Not much of a life for a girl who came
from nobody's love and in need of a home.

Little you knew of what could have been yours –
the first flirtation, the carefree dance;
your childhood was over before you grasped
the joys and burdens of innocence.
I stare at your picture in black and white,
wide-eyed and fresh yet tense with a frown
that betrays the presence of pain unborn;
a daughter caught in a world of her own
when death broke more than the dark earth's crust.

Then courtship and vows, and you became
a woman chosen for motherhood;
not many to guide you or even explain
those aches in the heart not understood
by child or man, and are carried alone.
Who but the bearer knows the cost
of parting with something so singly blessed
as the fruit of first labour? When the womb
and cradle share emptiness, love suffers most.

I see you now beyond that winter night,
when the farm, the cot, and death of a son
have faded again into candlelight.
The look in your eyes remains unchanged,
holding not one but a thousand years
of sorrow for all who have ever known
that proud dream of morning, when earth
promised more than the stars could show,
and hope sang like a lark in the girl's mouth.

DEATH OF AN UNCLE

(for Jack Alster)

The Marconi of the brickyards,
a radio-ham who spent his hours
between work-shifts probing
the wavelengths of the world,

lay there that morning like
a burnt-out valve, his ears
and nostrils plugged with cotton-wool,
his eyes forever fixed on distant stars.

Death was more honourable
and private then. The body
kept and guarded in the house
by loved-ones or the next-of-kin.

But I remember him all headphones
knobs and frequencies,
tracking an earthquake in Japan
or cries for help from sad Hungarians

terrorised by Russian tanks.
He was a genius at picking up
assassinations and rebellions
before the BBC got wind of them –

a gifted medium at a séance
calling dry voices from the air.
We all grew tense with expectation
as he repeated, 'Are you there?'

But when one night the world called him
he did not reply. The static
crackled in deaf ears, the stars
were frozen in his eyes.

THE INHERITOR

He will go on ploughing
even when his fields are no longer there,
when the last furrow
has been turned and buried under the weight
of a greedy city,
and the sun admits it has given up earth
like a lost child.

But he who year after year
fashioned the clods of his land to bear fruit
(counting them like sheep
as he went to sleep on his dying farm)
will turn over the shares
even when the day's light no longer shines
on the coulters' steel.

It will not be because
he has failed in his skills or love of the soil,
but because nature
(that quirky mistress with an ace up her sleeve)
will have decided
that he has held the tenancy long enough,
so the deal is up.

Reclaimed from water
the fields will return either to swamp, or go
down under concrete,
fertile only for noise and the brash substitutes
that a soul needs –
faith in the neon-lights and pleasures that pall
when a heart dies.

He is not a man to shed tears,
yet I know the sorrow he will feel when days
are not as he wished,
riding over the acres of a world that was
not only his breath
but the land that his father and fathers had farmed
and is no longer his..

69

THE WIRELESS AERIAL

(for David Twigg)

Twice as high as the clothes-line,
it went from pole to pole like rigging
over the deck of our garden.

Because of it we could hear people
speaking in London and Big Ben tolling
silence for the evening news.

There wasn't much that aerial couldn't do –
music, plays and comedians filled up the house
like favourite relatives.

How words which were invisible
came through the air to drop the world
right on our doorstep puzzled me.

But pole to pole was nearer to the truth
than we perceived. One Sunday morning
came the thin dry voice of Neville Chamberlain.

We sat in autumn stillness round the room
as mourners waiting for a funeral.
I felt our aerial had let us down.

Yet what I now remember most
is not the war, the sirens, or the bombs,
but how a blackbird always sang

from the tall and rough-hewn mast
high as our roof, its notes vibrating
in a clear blue glass of sky.

He and the blossom on the garden wall
became a well of indescribable delight
from which those echoes now return.

And nothing can destroy that world
though words remain as difficult to find
as wavelengths lost among the stars.

NEW YEAR'S EVE – 1997

(In memory of a brother who died 5.12.97.)

It was more than an old year
   giving way to the new;
such boundaries are questionable.
   Yet we still need
those moments to divide the days
   left empty now by friends
for whom raised glasses did not bring
   the lusty greetings
of a midnight bell. This year
   the silence picked on you.

You never were the rowdy reveller
   but preferred to see
the waiting hand slide imperceptibly
   across the hour,
more like a move you'd make in chess;
   not that you valued
any less another year brought in
   without indulgences.
Your death out-played mortality
   and kept our game in check.

As boys we were as strangers
   in the same small house,
sharing a room, a bed, and all those fears
   that childhood knows.
Yet we were different. I fought
   against submission
whilst you surrendered calmly to become
   a shadow on the wall
until all wrath was spent. I saw in you
   the Quaker then unborn.

It was through distances that we
    grew close, after
we'd left that long confining street
    to go beyond
the place where love was something more
    than we had understood.
It gave us freedom to become the friends
    our blood-ties made complete.
That was the gift your dying made us lose
    when wisdom came too late.

So as the midnight bell rang out
    its hammer blows
upon the changing year, I felt again
    the emptiness that comes
each time we raise those glasses
    which cannot be refilled.
Between our revelries a shadow passed
    that left a sudden chill,
like someone creeping quietly out of bed
    before the night is through.

THAT PLACE, THOSE HOURS

(In Memoriam – F.R.)

I did not think to write an elegy for you –
a friend whom I'd not seen for forty years,
until a boy passed by with sun-burnt skin
and from the sky a lark spilt notes of rain.

Then I remembered one hot summer day
when we played cricket in long meadow grass,
where cows stood watching every eager run
you notched in chalk upon your mellow blade.

I bowled for hours, shirt off, and unaware
of how the heat was blistering my back,
whilst you hit out, reluctant to declare
until you'd equalled Bradman's highest knock.

Then when my innings came I had the luck
to be distracted by a lark that rose
as your late-swinger hit my middle stump.
I claimed "no ball" but you'd hear none of that.

The hurt was worse than any peeling skin
and lasted for a month, or maybe more.
And so we parted company, still friends,
but never to recall our epic match.

Now houses crouch like fielders in the slips,
the grass is gone and there's no room to bat;
and you, I hear, at sixty have been caught
whilst I, amazingly, am still not out.

That place, those hours, the summer I thought lost,
were all brought back because a boy passed by
stripped to the waist and, from a heap of stones,
a new bird rose to haunt an empty sky.

A CHANGE IN THE CLIMATE

One day the waters will force us back
to where we belong, to the estranged hills
and abandoned farms that our forefathers
were driven from by a landlord's greed.

But our songs will not be of returning,
nor of those sorrows in a place where blood
darkened the soil when men were manacled
to a land fashioned out of an old flood.

We shall sing first of those skies that loomed
over our harvests, remembering neighbours
who, for five generations, made art
out of fields through the pains of their labour.

We shall think too of the fear in their hunger
and of those women who bore their children
to rise from despair and one fine morning
walk through the gates of an open border.

When the sea refuses the rivers, when dykes
no longer contain the waters that pour down
from high country, we shall lock our doors
for the last time and trek back to old hearthstones,

some to the west, others to the north, each
obeying those routes when the blood recalls
where the first couples met, where the hills promised
something their love thought was paradise.

And then we shall sing because, for their sakes,
we will have finished the journey.   It will not be
the fire or sword but the returning waters
that will end our exile and bring us home.

WAR-CEMETERY – POLAND

There are several reasons for sunflowers.
In isolation they are like scarecrows
stranded in English gardens, their heads
lolling from side to side, with no sense
of where the next day's sun will rise.
They show a heavy weariness, as if
their thoughts outweighed the wish
to stand upright.   It is a poor disguise
which, clown-like, makes the owners smile
to see them lean half-drunk against the fence.

Others, more free to tantalise the wind,
sway in large fields and openly display
a furnace of bright gold – flames
twisting across the earth to praise
the joy of warmth and surge of summer light.
One day their seeds will ooze sweet oil
and wise uplifted heads still turn
to follow the sun's downfall into night.
Child-like, they'll see each timely death
as a brief darkness wedged between long days.

But I remember now another scene
where they grew solemnly on soldiers' graves,
sunflowers reaching for the great sun's rays
as if to give back life to those below;
each head benevolent with hope
for limbs that could not move.   What saves
a man from his perpetual night
more than the promise of his soul's escape?
Erect, and for inspection dressed,
they stood unbowed, where wounds no longer show.

76

GOOD FRIDAY – SPAIN

It could have been here
where creation ran out of ideas,
that the shaped tree was dragged
through the shouting crowds
for a man to prove how faith
can survive even a pierced side.

There is little to show now
in the stones and ungathered thorns
how death was prolonged one afternoon
so that a town could celebrate
with fireworks and trumpets
its liberation from the threat of love.

But listen, and in the April wind
you'll hear his timeless words
haunting this wilderness – *Father,
forgive.* And from the one tree
not yet demolished by developers,
blossoms a flower, red as blood.

END OF TERM

They are gathering in rows upon the grass,
each class now posing for its photograph;
children assembled neatly into years
they'll never see again. Some laugh,
some try a permanent smile, all
caught for this last moment in an age
that will remind them of a day that was.

They know today their school is breaking up
for summer holidays but not, when they return,
how they'll have changed – for nothing stays
as timeless as the grins they're offering
to the camera. Soon they will learn
to smile in far more subtle ways,
for innocence, like childhood, does not keep.

So watching them this morning I can see
beyond the undeveloped film what each
child will become some twenty years away –
stressed-out and wondering how to cope
with their own offspring for so many weeks.
Will they then take this print of former days
to search in vain for something yet to be?

The classes now disperse and, one by one,
the boys and girls rejoicingly go home,
leaving not emptiness where laughter was
but ageless ghosts upon the uncut grass.
Each year I see a generation last
for three brief terms before the shutters close.
And always something more than age is lost.

FEELING EARTH PAUSE

The hour of long shadows over grass
        has its own stillness;
the sky, cloud-clear as glass, would
        if flicked by the wind's finger,
            ring as a fine goblet;
perfection perched on the stem of evening.

Somewhere between shadow and light
        a lark sings as though
his task was in the making of stars
        before earth slips like a spark
            from the sun's grasp,
leaving us only with a drained cup.

There are sounds other than those last notes
        of a bird that will itself
turn into a star.   Sheep with sore throats
        baa from the hills, their cries
            unchanged since Time began,
their language pitched always about one word.

And for a moment we, like the fields,
        hold our breath until
the shadows kneel down with the beasts,
        feeling earth pause on its axis
            as if it too needed
its own stillness to fold day within dark.

IN AN ALIEN HEAVEN

Suddenly, in the sea-blue sky, a lark sang,
and there were no longer stones at my feet
but grass that had given its dew to the heat
of the sun a lifetime ago, and nothing
can bring back the past with such swiftness of joy
as the song of that bird, nor will the boy
be forgotten though his days are diminishing.

Suddenly, there in an alien heaven,
where hills obscured the sky-line, a sound
so exquisite was heard from the pebbled ground
that I was granted a second chance even
to rise from the grass I had known as a child
and dance, as if all my years had been whiled
away in that place where the first joy was given.

EXPERIENCE

I am only just beginning to find the answers
when it's almost too late to ask the questions.

It's like being told I can fly when my wings
have been clipped to make flight impossible.

I find it most inconsiderate of life
to be blessed with such wisdom in one's old age.

Imagine, all that learning gone up in smoke
before we pass through the gates of the crematorium

*New Poems
(1999-2001)*

FIRST THINGS

You cannot wash away the colour of memory.
All day and night the rain has beaten on the house
and wiped out hills as if they were not there.

Although my eyes sought refuge then in sleep,
the scenes returned from their far distances –
familiar faces, fields, a broken fence.

Even the greyness of those first things did not fade:
the narrow streets that were afraid of light,
the over-crowded rooms, the roofs of slate.

Soon I could see how close those houses were,
the smoking chimneys and the brickyard kilns
beyond the town, whose fires will not go out.

And then my mother ran across the road, to give
a beggar tea where he stood drenched with rain.
It was an unpretentious act, almost like love.

There everything began – birth, fear and joy,
and all the deep complexities that sway
the ebb of days when we're no longer young.

We thought it was so simple once to live
where hours required no explanation,
no need to justify an impulse of the heart.

A MOTHER LOOKING
FOR HER CHILDREN

I see you now, a distraught bird
searching for her young, those weak
fledglings who, less than an hour ago,
half flew, half fell, from their small nest,
putting faith in wings that had no time to show
if they would ever reach some beckoning tree
beyond the claws of cat or hawk or crow.

You pass beyond the garden-fence and gate
looking for the family you'd lost – one
in his infancy before flight stood a chance,
one in his middle years with destinations
almost in his grasp, and one who fell
against the grain, forgetting all
you taught her when she was a girl.

I see you running down the street
asking the neighbours if they'd seen
your children who had not come home.
It's unlike them, you say, *where have they gone?* –
forgetting two were buried and the oldest one
inhabited a world now all her own.
What shadow crossed the night when they were born?

You go beyond the town into the fields,
calling against the wind until you think
the stars are children playing hide-and-seek
like birds among the hedgerows of the sky.
Night leaves you lonely and the years confuse.
I feel you weep not only for the lost but those
still to be caught by cat or hawk or crow.

VISITING HOUR

It was like a tower of Babel
but one where all those living there
spoke the same secret language –

Molly shouted to an empty chair
I-love-you-I-love-you-I-LOVE-YOU,
her long arms clutching at thin air,

while Maureen chanted loud enough to hear
(though no one listened any more)
silly-bugger-silly-bugger-he's-not-there.

And on t.v. in SONGS OF PRAISE
the earnest congregation sang
How sweet the name of Jesus sounds

as Clive attacked the locked front door
with blasphemies, then cried
why won't You let me out of here?

So one more Sunday-visit passed
as residents played solitaire
with memories we could not share.

And you, my dear, who once knew
all the family, sat in a corridor
talking to shadows, with no idea

that I now held your hand, your face
so drawn and old you made me see
our mother staring at the kitchen fire.

But she was wise enough to know
each heart has its own boundaries
and would, as I do, weep for you.

FEATHERS

He sat plucking a chicken. Not because
he wanted to but because my father
had no stomach for the job himself.

So I stood watching my grandfather
strip with some skill those feathers from a bird
wedged upside-down between his knees.

Five minutes earlier he'd wrung its neck,
stretched and twisted it as if it were
a skein of wool for someone else to knit.

The feathers came out easier if the flesh
was warm, before each quill had time
to set within the puckering skin.

He knew this was the only meat we'd get
that week to put upon our table,
so made his hands pursue their needful act.

Then when he shoved the feathers in a sack
a few escaped and floated in the air –
white flakes of down that settled on my back

and are still there.

LOSERS

I misunderstood you. For all those years
you, too, were trying to improve the hand
you had been dealt, or contradict the stars'
predictions, but they were fixed and would not bend.

Even your Sunday-suit was worn to show
the man inside his labourer's clothes could be
well-dressed in starched white shirts and velvet bow.
You courted flair if not flamboyancy.

I thought at times the image out of place;
your dreams lacked vision and your courage fire.
But I was wrong. Remembering your face
I see the disappointment hiding there.

Your own ambitions never had the luck
to win the game you tried so hard to play.
Your low cards seldom took a trick
and in the end you chose to throw away.

Now I have reached the age you were, I know
why there were times we two could never meet.
There was a joker in the pack who knew
you did not have the nerve or guile to cheat.

Forgive me if I sometimes thought you weak
or slow to find the words that would have healed.
I feel those moments now more deeply ache
and learn too late it was not you who failed.

BECAUSE OF LIFE OR DEATH

The woman who lived next door to us
lay dying of cancer in her front room.

It annoyed her that every afternoon
I had to practise on my cornet for an hour.

I hoped the melodies would ease her pain
but she complained and knocked upon the wall:

If you must play that thing don't choose
'We'll gather lilacs in the Spring again.'

My mother said, 'It would be better if today
we went to get some more corn for the chickens ...

'Life must go on and if they are not fed
as sure as eggs are eggs they'll never lay.'

I put my cornet back into its case.
Because of life, or death, I never learnt to play.

SHOPPING-DAYS

Who are they – these strangers
wearing the faces of the dead?
Out of the crowd I see a friend
coming towards me and increase my step.
Before the embarrassment of speech
his double turns away, fearing I'll ask
some crass, impertinent question,
or beg some money for a cup of tea.

Today the town is full of unknown persons,
yet every now and then a face appears
with all the features of a woman loved,
the eyes of one who had a special gift
for turning loneliness into a feast,
a smile that no one else could match;
and in an instant expectations lure
our footsteps to pursue them anxiously.

Last week I saw my brother cross the street
and ran to treat him to a drink,
remembering the night we tried to catch
the last bus home, the back of it
just always out of reach. I called
but in the noise could not be heard
and so stopped running, for neither he
nor I would ever get there now.

Perhaps it is the dead who come
to tease us on our shopping-days
and hide behind those masks to test
our consciences. If so, they'll see
what every crowd betrays –
an hunger in sad eyes, a love
the living cannot always give, the search
for something more than daily bread.

TWO MINIATURES

1. View from a Sick-bed

My window is a Jackson Pollock canvas
of bare branches, a black entanglement
of scars against a winter sky. I cannot see
where trees begin or twigs drip into non-existences.

And then an elongated sun closes its coffin-lid
on one more afternoon. A crow paces the day's hearse
out of town with the precision of a funeral. I'd
almost sell my soul to smell that air, pick up dead sticks.

2. Outlook

If I wanted to know the hour of my death
I would not go to a prophet or astrologer
but to a weather-forecaster, because there's
every chance that he, or she, might get it
wrong, making it later rather than sooner,
turning my depression into a high, at least
for the foreseeable future. And who knows
what sort of change that could bring about?
The low front now approaching from the west
could miss me altogether.

LOOK AT YOURSELF

You are sometimes coming too close to the silences
when there is no hair to brush back
and a skull stares at you with reproach, saying –

You had your chances but thought you could outwit love,
deceive even those presences you felt
hovered in air, as if you were a favourite child.

But one day you will go too far to satisfy that ghost
who haunts you most when you are unaware.
There'll be no tears to pay for your disgrace.

A hand will reach to switch the light on and discover
a face too white with grief to beg for pardon.
Cold eyes will be where stars were, and the mirror bare.

THE MIRROR

We nearly all come to it in the end.
I do not mean the death which is inevitable
but the place, how ever secret or well-known,
where we must be alone and stand as one
looking into a mirror for the first time.

And there should be an hour when no one else
disturbs the holding of earth's breath,
for this is when we see beyond the glass
and find the fragments now become the whole;
our several faces stripped of their disguise.

There can be moments when such stillness fills
a room we think we've always known.
Then suddenly a salt-glazed chalice used
to hold a plant now overflows with wine;
an alabaster jar itself becomes the balm.

Today a mirror held a ghostly form
half-strange yet half-familiar. I tried
to touch his arm but when my hand reached out
my own arm rose to bar me from the frame;
and there was nothing where once two had been.

THE FLITTING

I've left my own old home of homes
John Clare

It was all very well for you, Clare,
sitting there for five days in your new home
writing a poem about leaving Helpston,
but who did the unpacking? Patty, I suppose,
always on hand to pick up the pieces,
not that there would have been much
in the way of furniture – your favourite chair,
a table, some pots and pans, your books
and that engraving by de Wint, all
you could stack on to a handcart
borrowed from a neighbour …
                              And so you went,
trailing your past to Northborough, a man
torn up by the roots, all spirit spent.

I think I know how you felt, though I
did my own unpacking and helped unload
the van that brought us to this house in Wales.
And unlike you, it was my native scene
that had grown strange, the ageing sun
uncertain of which field to shine upon,
                              the lark song gone.
Now I must wait to hear how words will sound
where hills demand a greater share of sky,
aware that what my eyes will miss cannot be gauged
in miles, that maybe you were right to say
leaving one box unpacked is always wise.

CREDENHILL

(for Ronald Blythe)

We arrived, expecting the door to be locked.
Set back from the main road, the church was not
one to attract those against whom keys are turned.

Yet by a gift of chance we found it open
and, when we stepped inside, it was as if we'd crossed
three centuries, for there before the altar

stood the man who'd beckoned us this far –
Traherne, the poet-priest, sharing the sacrament
with one who knelt alone, as if he'd never ceased

in breaking of the bread, or consecrating wine.
And yet we knew the day had half-deceived
for there was evidence of more troubled times –

outside were graves of Polish airmen
who'd died in exile when our age
turned its back on a benevolent sun.

Having assumed the church would not admit
two travellers, we were surprised to find
the altar candles lit, and hear the language

of the Eucharist, not spoken for effect
but offered in remembrance of One for whom
the gentle poet sang when he was celebrant.

We stayed until the Service reached its end –
two watching two and each aware
of someone other being there – a presence

strangely meant, allowing us a glimpse
of one man's vision of *immortal wheat*
which never should be reaped nor was ever sown.

CLOSER TO ICE THAN FIRE

(for David and Danielle)

The last hour of sunlight reddens
the bark of a 5000-year-old yew tree
until it is the colour of raw flesh
cracked by frost or grief's proximity.
Flakes of dry skin litter the grass
and I am left to ponder on an age
that gave this titan its first Spring.

What bird or windfall dropped that seed
three thousand years before an unknown star
paused for a moment over Bethlehem?
Its birth-time passed even before Akhenaten
worshipped the sun, or the coming of those
who chose these Welsh hills for their buryings.
Among the dead it's still a living thing.

Before ghosts were born or stones carved
with our epitaphs, it heard the first sheep
bleat on the hills and the first shepherds
calling to their flocks over the deep
valleys before language was divided.
It is almost as old as sleep, almost
as old as the first tale ever told.

But neither Adam nor Eve would claim it
as part of their garden. It was not designed
to comfort those fallen from grace.
It is a survivor, a colossus left behind
by a cold star, closer to ice than fire.
Its fruit offers no joy to the tongue –
the seeds more fatal than any sin.

Yet there it stands, heavy with its past
of sword-rust, plagues, famine and holocausts.
Each ring within its girth records
some tyrant, massacre, saint or martyrdom.
I do not know which age I would fear most
for with the sun's last spear-thrust I can see
tomorrow caught already in the tree.

A WELSH HILL

It is the heart within the hill
that makes it more than a hill, the pulse
of millions of years that has fed the springs
and veins within the rocks, or the grass
waiting to rise from its sad battleground.
So much of earth's kind has wept,
worked and perished on its maternal thighs.

It is an island, half-removed
yet part of the whole; a shy continent.
See how small all things are that try
to survive on its ribbed sides year after year;
a button-row of cows divides a field,
a tractor trickles like a drop of blood
down from the wound made by a dragged plough.

It is as perfect as anything
in nature can be perfect; shape, size,
distance and its sleeping silence keeping at bay
a world rapacious to exploit its virtues –
developers, speculators, seekers of status,
and those for whom nature is always
a commercial proposition awaiting an opportunity.

This hill has been fought over
for centuries and there are some evenings
when the light makes it so timelessly mellow
that we can see it sigh with the memories
of lost farms, wars, or petty arguments
and the tears that followed from those
who were, as always, mostly innocent.

But there are some mornings
when the mist rises from its shawled back
that we know those perpetual springs will nourish
the unborn grass, that new sheep and cattle
will graze down to the roots of our history
as brief as a day in the eyes of the rocks;
that this hill will survive all greed, grief, fire, snow.

A VALEDICTION

for all who lay under the stars
Edward Thomas

It has come to this:
there is only the one dead who can
at any time receive
the silence and respect for all the millions
who deserve remembrance.
And circumstance today has chosen you –
Catherine Edwards, who died two centuries ago.

The churchyard's full of daffodils
and there are poorer graves than yours
that lean to eavesdrop on those words
which never can be shared
beyond the secrets of our consciences.
But you are now the one for whom
all elegies are sung or tears come true.

Here, by your stone, I think of those
who were my friends – that boy
of stammering speech, so fluent with his pen;
and he who, having fought with stars,
navvied among Welsh rocks
until the valleys filled with water
and the vexed farms drowned.

He spent his wages on a box of paints
then, out of untamed skies, made art.
And there was one who mourned
the land she lost more than the love
she'd never known from man or child.
I multiply each flower and find
yet more ghosts beckoning –

not least that lady whose fine house
offered me refuge, music, books,
who saw her own world slowly stripped
of meaning, unless those days are caught
in what the heart preserves of light.
Catherine, receive for them
this valediction of a grateful man.

A BALLAD OF TWO TREES

Adam and Eve walked over the hill –
'Where shall we go today?
We've already been to paradise
and were not allowed to stay.'

They went down to the valley
to find a room at the inn –
'Now we are clothed no one will know
of our original sin.'

But no one gave them shelter
and they couldn't afford a meal –
'If it goes on like this,' said Adam,
'I'm afraid we'll have to steal.'

They made their way to the city
where they slept in the sleepless street,
bewildered by the lurid lights
and a million wealthy feet.

'It's all your fault,' said Adam,
'for robbing that apple tree.'
'Not so,' said Eve, 'the blame is yours
for wanting more of me.'

They walked back to the country
like two sad refugees;
and the days soon turned to winter,
and the rivers began to freeze.

They climbed a hill and gazed on
the land that had been theirs –
'It's a wilderness,' Eve whispered,
'with nettles, weeds and tares.'

They rested on the hill-top,
frozen to death by the cold;
both white-haired and naked
and stiff with growing old.

In time Spring clothed their branches
with blossom and leaves of green,
to remind them again of paradise
and a world that might have been.

TAKING DOWN THE APPLE TREE

(for Mac and Ilona)

If Adam had done this in the first place
it would have saved us a lot of trouble.
And this is not a criticism of Eve
who would not have needed to steal the apple
if only he'd paid her more attention
instead of fretting over his brand-new garden.

It was because of the apple that she found out
she was naked. Now, thought she, if I
could get him to see me like this maybe
it would take his mind off more trivial matters.
And it did. He looked up one day from the seed
catalogue he was compiling and there stood
this beautiful woman with nothing on.

Hey! he thought. What have I been missing?
And when she asked if he would like to taste
the forbidden fruit, how could he refuse?
He ate right to the core (which he couldn't swallow)
and began to see that he, too, was naked.

Whether Eve would have had the same success
with a pomegranate or gooseberry, no one can say.
Sadly, their children brought them nothing
but misery, with murder, incest, greed
and treachery – which will explain why we
have bought a bird-bath to replace our tree.

NEIGHBOURHOOD WATCH

She arrives three times a week
to take afternoon-tea with her husband,
sitting close to his grave on the stone seat
placed there for that reason.

She brings his dog – now her dog –
who settles near his master's feet.
The grass around the rim is cut to look
as cosy as their favourite fireside rug.

She stays almost an hour,
breathing her thoughts, a silent tête-a-tête.
Convinced he's listening, she says again
how much she misses him at nights.

Then, when it's time to go,
she packs away the unseen cups and plates
which they once shared when love for them
was always so complete.

She does not know or care
if she is watched. This hour is intimate
for she is in that private world
where hearts still quicken when hands touch.

It is not her devotion
that is strange but the cold stare of those
who wait to see if, one day, she might cry
and leave a crushed, wet Kleenex on the seat.

DOUBLE EXPOSURE

(for David and Jay)

Two worlds in one and neither real.
One set of images imposed upon another,
making the prints surrealistic.

Because they're twice-exposed
the photographs betray our vain attempts
to catalogue a year. The seasons blur.

Autumn has trees of snow, while sheep
graze in our sitting-room. The sky
is quartered by a dry-stone wall.

Gravestones crouch in the shrubbery
and greetings-cards are strung upon a hill
where angels hang-glide, dressed in red and blue.

Now any ghost could pass our five-barred gate
which has itself become a wintry wraith.
(The two-dimensional is only partly fake.)

The church is so transparent we can see
beyond its porch to where an ancient site
was used for pagan rituals.

A light burns dimly on the altar stone
and there are figures lurking in the dark
who would rewind their seasons, given chance.

The spoilt film served some purpose, I suppose.
Beneath the images we try to make
are those that keep resurfacing to shock.

THE SILENCE OF NANTGWYLLT *

They come to look at the water,
to walk paths designed to make a place look natural,
or trek through woodlands coaxed into a landscape
    where nature too is checked.

The dam's stone walls are as cathedrals
open to the sky, their great roofs gone.
There is a stillness on the lake as if
    it could be walked on, its light skin-tight.

For some it is enough to take the guide-book trail
or tread the tourist-routes. Others
may pause to watch the kite
    rise high above their cameras' reach.

Beneath the water lies a world, hidden
like artefacts in a museum-case –
farms, cottages, a school – their names
    now listed in a public records book.

Deep under Caban Coch are paths
where Shelley ran with Harriet
and spent his summers in a house
    that rang with his exuberant wit.

Nantgwyllt went silent before this reservoir
made sure those paths did not become
a hallowed track when he was drowned
    in an Italian bay – a pre-run of its fate.

Years separate the waters.
Yet something stays – a question
touching all who find more than a dam –
    a guilt perhaps that will not go away.

*   *a house in the Elan Valley where Shelley stayed and*
    eventually hoped to live.

ELEGY FOR A RHONDDA MAN

After forty years of forgetting why
in a strange land
you were proud of your own country,
I have returned,
not as a visitor to verify your claims
but to share in the memory
of those who kept you company –
the men you worked with,
the streets that echoed with their names.

It was not then as now, where flocks of sheep
spill down the hills
like sea-foam spread by waves that break
and then recede.
They are dispersed, re-formed, made fleece again
as if to mock the constant pull
of death's dull bell. Your valleys bred
a harsher life
of narrow hopes and colder rain.

It was a world of darkness, coal and sweat
where winter-shifts
deprived you of a whole day's light.
Often you'd say
'there's not a place on earth where blood
has never fed the roots
of grass or stained the helpless rocks
for someone's gain.'
And yet, deep down, this place for you was good.

So I have come to raise those buried years
        and all the men
who were your heroes, either in life
        or in the books
you read each night by candlelight –
        Nietzsche, Spinoza and Tom Paine,
and those who vanished from an age
        where words were deeds,
believing fervently their cause was right.

I think of how your longing would be healed
        now by this land –
the bracken turning and the trees
        clutching their tithes
for Michaelmas. See how the proud
        hawk stays poised in the air
as if it were a star hung between clouds,
        how sheep now pile
like wind-drift by a wall time cannot break.

These are the moments you would come to know,
        your work-days done.
I see you on the bwlch, your pit-prop back
        shedding the weight
of forty years spent in the dark until
        your eyes flinched at the sun.
Now all those scars are gone, your limbs
        at last unchained,
and you become a man again on your own hill.

PORTRAIT OF AN ARTIST

(i.m. John Hutton)

He became one of his own paintings –
a closed door hidden in shadow,
or a bare tree in a field of snow.

He was part fact and part imagination
disguising what we wished to see
with what he wanted us to know.

He was both form and abstract –
a public figure, often debonair,
a late Bohemian we had to share.

He hid behind each sable stroke
or daring gesture from his palette-knife,
hoping we'd not recognise despair.

He much preferred to play the joker then
whose tricks could still deceive
though we had seen them many times before.

We knew within his paintings he had tried
to camouflage the scars of war –
the pain of fire, the falling from cold air.

Yet sometimes he was sunlight on old stone,
a shaper of the seasons who could fill
a canvas stretched from miles of sky

and make the emptiness vibrate
with what he saw beyond earth's rim.
He knew how distance could outstrip the eye.

But when it came to dying, he believed
it was a private view and went alone,
became the door, the shadow and the snow –

an enigmatic man not willing to unveil
the finished portrait for his friends to see,
and who he was no one will ever know.

THE PALES

Snow on the hills and a raw wind
threading the eye of the lane's needle –
that narrow track cracking with ice
on the threadbare back of winter.

The latched gate, shackled with frost,
resisted opening, as if our presence
was not welcome. We felt as strangers
who were being watched,

for we were there on impulse
not a pilgrimage – a sudden spur
changing our route to bring us
to that small thatched Meeting-house.

The dull door was not locked. Inside,
one room suggested that, unseen,
a congregation was still sitting there –
a calm society of ghosts

where all were equal and each one
as sacred as the earth on which,
three centuries ago, this house was built –
remoteness then best suited for God's few.

Here peace was settled in the mind
without vain words. Beneath the dust
were fragments always left behind –
the smell of faith, the finger-prints of prayer.

We stood and watched our breath become
part of its breath. Now we were numbered
with the many who had found
a moment's refuge from soul's fear.

Outside, we faced the pricking wind
until the flesh felt pain enough to bleed.
But no coat's warm enough against the cold
bred by a disbelieving world.

Close by, beneath dark trees, old graves
leaned in their silence towards Pen-y-Bont.
And we, descending through the fields,
sought in the snow a more familiar route.

ENDGAME

Forget the trumpets. The stadium is empty
except for some old codgers who now sit
talking about those peerless days when it
was possible to applaud true artistry.
Then there wore skills, the rules were still obeyed
and every trick was recognised by those
who knew the finest players always chose
perfection over thrills. Not much has stayed.

Today the crowds have gone elsewhere to find
more dazzling entertainment and admire
. pretenders who desire wealth and fame.
But soon they will be scattered by the wind,
their songs as letters thrown upon a fire
and silence, too, forget them, name by name.